HEINEMANN STATE STUDIES

All Around California

Regions and Resources

Mir Tamim Ansary

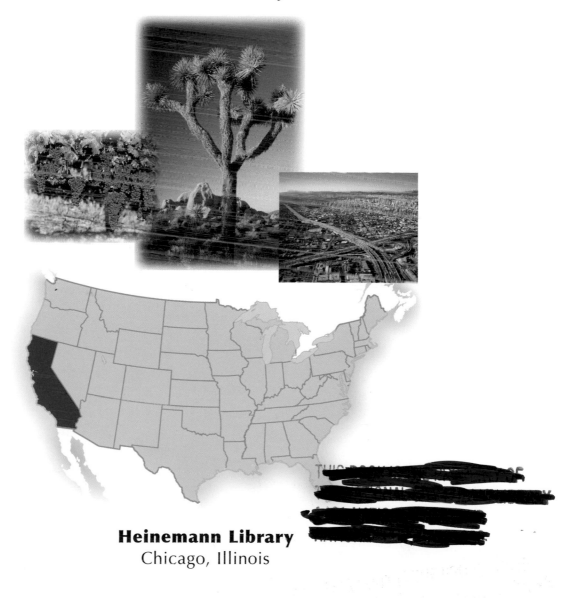

Heinemann Library
Chicago, Illinois

Designed by Heinemann Library
Page layout by Depke Design
Printed and bound in the United States by
 Lake Book Manufacturing, Inc.

07 06 05 04 03
10 9 8 7 6 5 4 3 2 1

Library of Congress
Cataloging-in-Publication Data
Ansary, Mir Tamim.
  All around California : regions and resources /
by Mir Tamim Ansary.
    p. cm. -- (State studies)
Includes bibliographical references and index.
  ISBN 1-40340-339-2 (hardcover)
ISBN 1-4034-0556-5 (pbk.)
  1. California--Geography--Juvenile literature.
I. Title. II. State studies
(Heinemann Library (Firm))
  F861.8 .A47 2002
  917.94--dc21

2002010284

Acknowledgments
The author and publishers are grateful to the following for permission to reproduce copyright material:

Cover photographs by (top, L-R) Bob Ecker/Heinemann Library, Charles E. Rotkin/Corbis, Joel W. Rogers/Corbis, Yann Arthus-Bertrand/Corbis (main) Gerald French/Corbis

Title page (L-R) Bob Ecker/Heinemann Library, Galen Rowell/Corbis, Bill Ross/Corbis; contents page Galen Rowell/Corbis; pp. 4T, 26, 27B, 44 Nik Wheeler/Corbis; pp. 4B, 9, 11T, 27T Bob Ecker/Heinemann Library; pp. 5, 7, 10, 12, 14, 28, 30, 33, 36, 38, 41, 43, 45 maps.com/Heinemann Library; p. 6 Neil Rabinowitz/Corbis; p. 11B Joel W. Rogers/Corbis; p. 13 Morton Beebe/Corbis; pp. 15, 31T Spencer Grant/Photo Edit; pp. 16, 39B Phil Schermeister/Corbis; p. 17T Roger Ressmeyer/Corbis; pp. 17B, 39T Ed Kashi/Corbis; p. 18 Mark Richards/Photo Edit; p. 19 Jonathan Blair/Corbis; p. 20 Joseph Sohm/ChromoSohm Inc./Corbis; p. 21T Joseph Sohm/Visions of America/Corbis; p. 21B Richard Cummins/Corbis; p. 22 Charles E. Rotkin/Corbis; p. 23 Jan Butchofsky-Houser/Corbis; p. 24 Robert Holmes/Corbis; p. 25 Bill Ross/Corbis; p. 29 Mark Downey; p. 31B Ecoscene/Corbis; p. 32 Yann Arthus-Bertrand/Corbis; p. 34 Wolfgang Kaehler/Corbis; pp. 35, 40 Galen Rowell/Corbis; p. 37 Philip James Corwin/Corbis; p. 42 Darrell Gulin/Corbis

Photo research by Bobbie Schultz

Thanks to expert reader, author, and editor, Marlene Smith-Baranzini, M.A., for her help in the preparation of this book. Also, special thanks to Lucinda Surber for her curriculum guidance.

Some words are shown in bold, **like this.** You can find out what they mean by looking in the glossary.

Contents

An Introduction to California 4

The Northern Coast 9

The Southern Coast 19

The Central Valley 29

The High Mountains 35

Desert and Basin 40

Map of California 45

Glossary 46

More Books to Read 47

Index 48

About the Author 48

An Introduction to California

In the United States, any traveler moving west eventually ends up in California. The only state west of California is Hawaii, a group of islands in the Pacific Ocean. A person heading south from California will cross the border into Mexico, a different country.

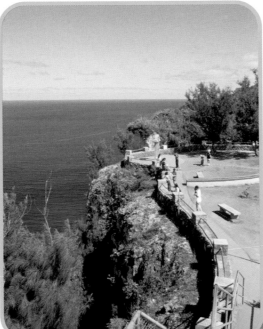

Alaska and Texas cover more land than California, but no state has more people. California has almost twice as many people as New York, the next biggest state in population.

Once you reach the Pacific Ocean coast, you are at the edge of the United States. According to the U.S. Census Bureau, about 35 million people lived in this warm, sunny area in 2002.

California Topography

High
Mountain

Goose
Lake

Arcata
Eureka

Shasta
Lake

Redding

Sacramento River

Sacramento

Lake
Tahoe

Mono
Lake

San Francisco Oakland

Coastal San Jose

San Joaquin River

Monterey

Fresno

Central
Valley

Tulare
Lake

Bakersfield

PACIFIC OCEAN

Santa Maria

Desert

Colorado River
Aqueduct

Santa Barbara

Los Angeles

Palm Springs

Long Beach

San Diego
Aqueduct

Salton
Sea

San Diego

N
W   E
S

0   100 mi.

14,495 ft ▸
12,500 ft ▸
10,000 ft ▸
7,500 ft ▸
5,000 ft ▸
2,500 ft ▸
Sea level ▸

+ Highest Elevation (14,495 ft.)
+ Lowest Elevation (282 ft.)
Death Valley

California is crowded because people have come to the state in such large numbers for so long. Four of the twenty biggest cities in the United States—Los Angeles, San Diego, San Jose, and San Francisco—are in California. However, some areas, such as Modoc County in the northeast, are nearly empty.

*California has many different types of **landforms.** There are mountains, valleys, forests, deserts, and a long coastline.*

Travel and **tourism** is a big business throughout the state of California. Each year, more than 50 million tourists come in from other states and countries. More

Mount San Jacinto and other snow-capped mountains are the background for the palm trees found in Palm Desert.

than one million Californians work in businesses that serve tourists. They drive tour buses, run restaurants and hotels, sell **souvenirs** and supplies, operate travel agencies, and so on. **Tourism** is worth $75 billion to the state each year, ranking as the third-largest state **industry.**

Earthquake Country

California sits on two great sheets of rock called plates. These plates float on a deeper layer of melted rock. Since the plates are separate, they can slip against each other. When they do, earthquakes jolt the ground above. California gets about 5,000 earthquakes each year. Most are too small to notice, but a few have been the biggest in U.S. history.

California Population

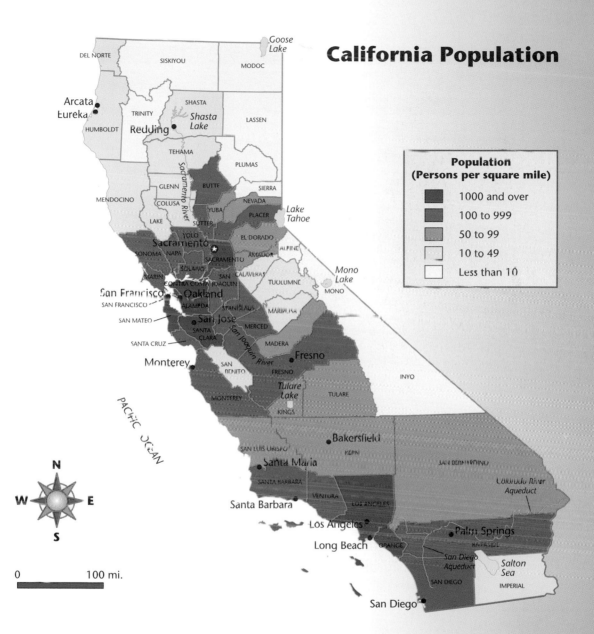

Population (Persons per square mile)

- 1000 and over
- 100 to 999
- 50 to 99
- 10 to 49
- Less than 10

0   100 mi.

THE LAND THAT IS CALIFORNIA

When looking at California from above, you would find it divided among several **landforms.** Tall mountains line the northern border of the state and much of the eastern border. Lower mountain ranges wrinkle the land along the West

California's population is concentrated around big cities such as Los Angeles and San Francisco. Desert and mountainous areas have fewer people.

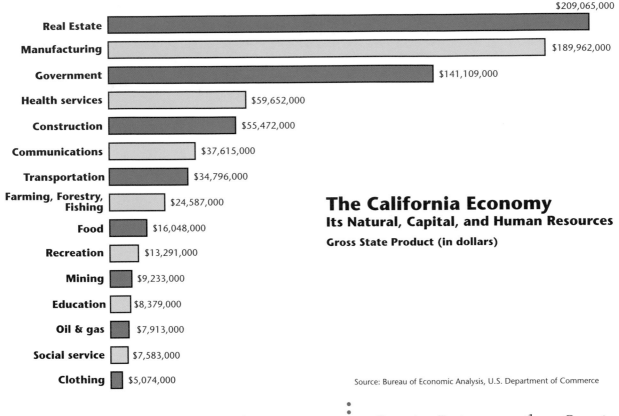

Real Estate	$209,065,000
Manufacturing	$189,962,000
Government	$141,109,000
Health services	$59,652,000
Construction	$55,472,000
Communications	$37,615,000
Transportation	$34,796,000
Farming, Forestry, Fishing	$24,587,000
Food	$16,048,000
Recreation	$13,291,000
Mining	$9,233,000
Education	$8,379,000
Oil & gas	$7,913,000
Social service	$7,583,000
Clothing	$5,074,000

The California Economy
Its Natural, Capital, and Human Resources
Gross State Product (in dollars)

Source: Bureau of Economic Analysis, U.S. Department of Commerce

This graph shows the amount of money generated by California workers who hold a variety of jobs.

Coast. Between the Coast Ranges and the Sierra Nevada range in the east lies a long, slipper-shaped plain called the Central Valley. There are also three neighboring deserts: the Mojave Desert, Death Valley, and the Colorado Desert.

Each region in California is unique. Each faces different challenges in meeting the needs of its population. Each region has varied **landforms** that affect the people who live there. Different **industries** employ many types of workers, and each region also offers different **recreational** opportunities as well. Cities are the heart of some regions, while vast, open spaces are found in others. Together, all of these regions create a state that is appealing to people of all ages and **ethnicities.** This state is California.

The Northern Coast

The land of the California coast varies from north to south. North of San Luis Obispo, the coast becomes more rugged. High hills rise directly from the water's edge. Narrow beaches are tucked between the hills, and big rocks rise out of the waters offshore. Barking seals and squawking gulls cover these rocks. Big Sur, the 60 or so miles of land between San Luis Obispo and Monterey Bay, is the most rugged part of the California coastline.

CLIMATE

The weather on the north coast is cool, but never bitterly cold. Light snow may dust the mountaintops at

In the central and north coast regions, mountain ranges run along the 1,264-mile coastline.

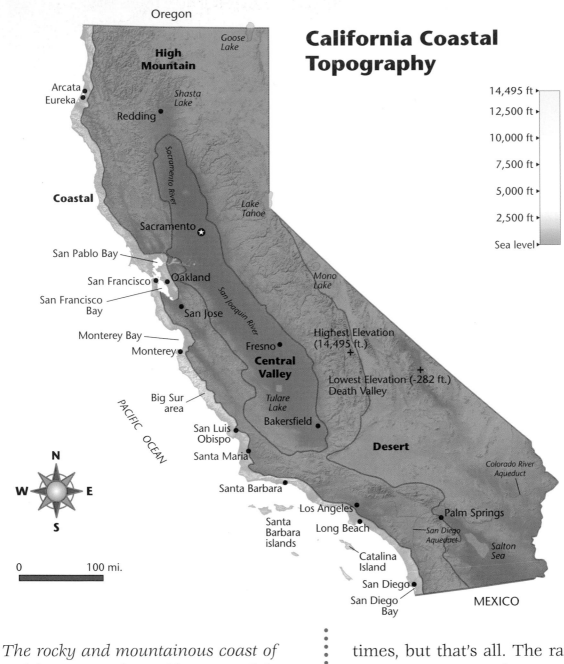

California Coastal Topography

Oregon

Goose Lake

High Mountain

Arcata
Eureka

Shasta Lake

Redding

Sacramento River

Coastal

Lake Tahoe

Sacramento

San Pablo Bay

San Francisco — Oakland

San Francisco Bay

San Joaquin River

Mono Lake

San Jose

Monterey Bay

Monterey

Fresno

Highest Elevation (14,495 ft.) +

Central Valley

Lowest Elevation (-282 ft.) + Death Valley

Big Sur area

Tulare Lake

Bakersfield

San Luis Obispo

Desert

Santa Maria

PACIFIC OCEAN

Santa Barbara

Colorado River Aqueduct

Los Angeles

Santa Barbara islands

Long Beach

Palm Springs

San Diego Aqueduct

Salton Sea

Catalina Island

San Diego

San Diego Bay

MEXICO

N
W   E
S

0   100 mi.

14,495 ft ▸
12,500 ft ▸
10,000 ft ▸
7,500 ft ▸
5,000 ft ▸
2,500 ft ▸
Sea level ▸

The rocky and mountainous coast of California was formed by natural forces such as volcanoes and earthquakes.

times, but that's all. The rainfall increases, too. Del Norte, the most northern county, gets an average of 80 inches a year! San Francisco's average summer temperatures are in the low 70s, yet winter temperatures rarely fall below freezing (32°F.)

FARMING

The north coast has many natural **resources** important to farmers. The valleys that cut through the coast range have excellent soil. This part of the coast also gets plenty of rain. North of Santa Cruz, fields of asparagus and other vegetables are visible from the road. North of San Francisco, many dairy farms produce eggs, milk, and cheese. The small city of Petaluma calls itself the egg **capital** of the world.

Grapes grown in California are used not only for wine, but to make raisins and be sold as fruit for eating.

The richest "farms" of coastal California **thrive** in the Napa and Sonoma Valleys. Almost all of these "farms" are **vineyards.** At one time, almost all of America's fine wines came from Napa Valley. Later, Sonoma began to rival Napa. Now, many states have wineries, but the wines from Sonoma and Napa still win many prizes.

Fishers catch king salmon on the north coast, a fish prized for its sweet meat. Divers may only gather abalone in the north, from San Francisco to the state line. This tasty shellfish is decreasing in population. People need a special fishing license to catch them.

Northern California is considered the salmon capital of the West Coast. Here, a fishing boat brings in the day's catch.

11

California Precipitation

Average Yearly Precipitation in Inches

96 to 127	■
80 to 96	■
64 to 80	■
48 to 64	■
32 to 48	■
24 to 32	■
16 to 24	■
8 to 16	■
0 to 8	□

0   100 mi.

The varied landscape of California affects the amount of rain each area receives. The deserts get very little rain, while the northern region is often wet and rainy.

SAN FRANCISCO

Crowded San Francisco covers one of the **peninsulas** that form the Golden Gate. It cannot grow larger because water surrounds it on three sides. Other cities, however, extend around the Bay. Each one merges into the next, with no real countryside in between. Berkeley sits across the Bay, east of San Francisco. It merges into Oakland in the south. Oakland gives way to a string of smaller cities. The **suburbs** of San Jose begin where the smaller cities end.

San Francisco grew up almost overnight during the gold rush of the late 1840s and early 1850s. Money still pours through it, because San Francisco is the financial center of the West Coast. The downtown area looks like a forest of banks. San Francisco is also an important **cultural** center. The city has the important Asian Art Museum, an opera company, a **symphony,** and a ballet.

Much of the city is built on steep hills that offer views of the ocean and bay. The San Francisco Bay is the biggest bay on the West Coast, and has a narrow mouth that makes it more like an **inland** sea. Two peninsulas form this mouth. Behind this mouth, the bay stretches both north and south. The northern branch is called the San Pablo Bay. The Sacramento River pours into the tip of it. The other branch, the San Francisco Bay, flows generally south about 60 miles.

Almost every house that survived the 1906 earthquake has been **preserved,** giving San Francisco a charming, historic feel. Many of these wooden houses are called "Victorians" because their style took shape when Queen Victoria ruled Great Britain. Many houses have **gables,**

Many of the neighborhoods in San Francisco have old Victorian homes like these. They are called "painted ladies" because of the beautiful detailing on them.

California Coastal Resources

Natural Resources

- Oil
- Natural gas
- Borax
- Limestone
- Gold, silver
- Sand, gravel

Manufacturing

- Computers
- Clothing

Industry

- Forest products
- Fruit
- Grapes
- Rice
- Vegetables
- Olives
- Dairy products
- Cotton
- Sugar beets
- Cattle
- Walnuts
- Poultry
- Fish
- Skiing

PACIFIC OCEAN

High Mountain
Arcata
Eureka
Redding
Sacramento
San Francisco
Oakland
Coastal
San Jose
Monterey
Fresno
Central Valley
Bakersfield
Santa Maria
Desert
Santa Barbara
Los Angeles
Palm Springs
Long Beach
San Diego

0   100 mi.

N W E S

The long coastal region provides many of California's resources, including fruits and vegetables, oil, forest products, and manufactured goods.

turrets, and **bay windows.** They are often painted in bright colors to make the decorations stand out. San Francisco's beauty is an **economic resource,** too, because it draws tourists to the city.

TOURIST ATTRACTIONS

San Francisco's interesting neighborhoods are also an economic resource. Chinatown, for example, has the look and feel of a city in China. North Beach is full of

Italian restaurants and coffee-houses. A famous group of poets called the Beats lived and worked there in the 1950s. Tourists still come to San Francisco to relive the Beat Era. Haight Ashbury is another famous neighborhood. The hippie movement of the 1960s was born there. Haight Street still looks much as it did in that time.

Cable cars run along two of San Francisco's streets. They are used mainly by tourists. Other attractions include the Golden Gate Bridge and Golden Gate Park. Also, more than 14 million travelers visit the Golden Gate National **Recreation** Area. This is a set of parks and woods that stretches from San Francisco into Marin. It gets the most paid visitors of any national park in the state.

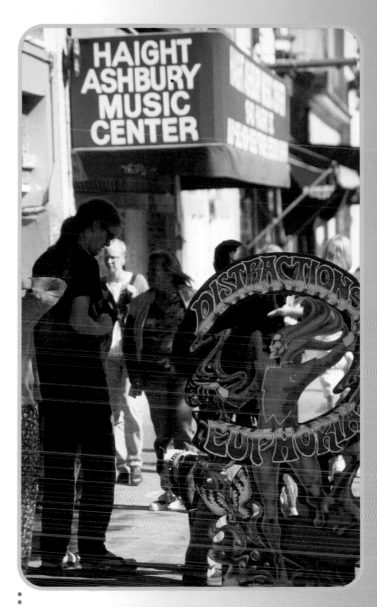

In the 1960s, Haight Ashbury was the center for music, painting, poetry, and literature.

THE SAN FRANCISCO BAY AREA

Several cities together make up the San Francisco Bay Area, the major **urban** center of the north. Berkeley revolves mainly around one **industry,** which is education. This town boasts the first and finest **campus** in the University of California system. Because of the university, a large number of the people in Berkeley are students. Many professors who teach at the school live in the hills above the campus.

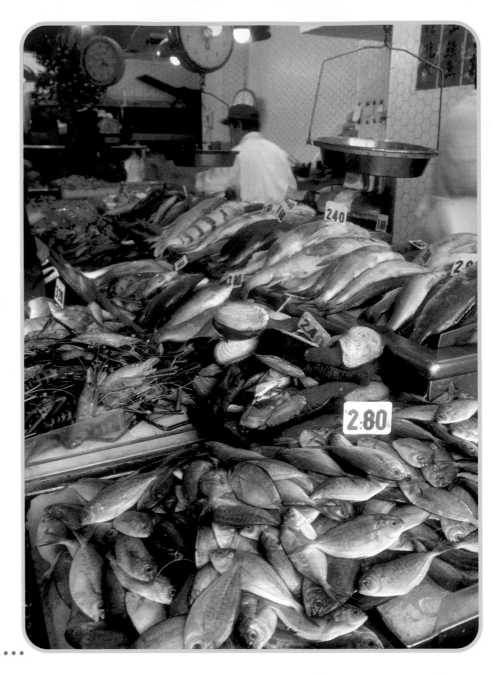

A variety of fish wait for sale at the Stockton Street Fish Market in San Francisco.

Oakland, by contrast, is often seen as less interesting by its Bay Area neighbors. It too has the old houses and the beautiful views, but it is a working city filled with small factories. Oakland's waterfront remains a working port, not a tourist's playground.

San Jose is not as well known as San Francisco, but it actually has more people. It is the biggest city in the Bay Area. For many years, it served as a **hub** for the farms of the Central Valley. Now, San Jose has stronger ties to the Bay Area computer **industry.**

Northern California does not have as many people as the southern part of the state. However, it does have several state and national parks and opportunities for outdoor **recreation,** including hiking, camping, and fishing.

Northern California is probably best known as the home of Silicon Valley, in Santa Clara County. Most computer companies have main offices in Silicon Valley, the area between San Jose and San Francisco.

High-tech machines and robots help to make parts for computers and other machinery. Below are the headquarters for the Oracle Corporation, located in Silicon Valley.

Other Northern California **industries** include the largest **bioscience** industry in the world and several important entertainment studios as well. Many special effects that you see in movies are made at Marin County's Industrial Light and Magic.

The Bay Area has many public transportation systems. Each city has its own bus system. Some commuters take ferries to San Francisco. They must then board a bus to get to their destination. Others ride the Bay Area Rapid Transit, also known as BART. Another system called Caltrans runs trains to the south Bay. The Golden Gate Transit runs buses to Marin. Amtrak trains stop in Oakland, and they carry passengers to and from distant cities. Most visitors, however, arrive by car or fly into one of the Bay Area's three airports.

*Bay Area Rapid Transit (BART) mainly connects downtown San Francisco to cities and **suburbs** east of the Bay.*

The Southern Coast

The southern coast is marked by long stretches of flat, sandy beach. A number of large islands, including the Santa Barbara Islands and Catalina Island, lie offshore. Set back from the beaches are rolling hills. These hills rise to mountain ranges.

Two large bays cut into the southern coast of California. Near the Mexican border is the San Diego Bay. It is a deep, narrow channel shaped like a candy cane. North of Big Sur is Monterey Bay, a wide curve shaped like a crescent moon. It is located about halfway between Mexico and the state of Oregon.

CLIMATE

Southwestern California has a Mediterranean **climate.** This means that rain falls only in the winter and the temperature is mild. Summers are warm but rarely get unpleasantly hot, because ocean breezes help to cool things off. Winters never get very cold. Storms drench

The Monterey Bay National Marine Sanctuary is a federally protected marine area offshore of California's central coast. It is home to fish, mammals, plants, invertebrates, and seabirds.

the coast at times, but the rain falls in short, heavy bursts. Southern California gets more days of sunshine than most of the world—over 300 days a year.

The **climate** of southern California is very pleasant, but it has created a problem, too. It has attracted too many people for the amount of water available. Rivers in southern California usually run dry in the summer.

A DRY AREA

The most important waterways are those made by people: long **canals** called **aqueducts.** The Los Angeles Aqueduct brings water from the Owens Valley in the Sierra Nevada. The Colorado Aqueduct brings water from the Colorado River. Near Los Angeles, the aqueduct branches into two waterways. One branch runs south to San Diego. Without aqueducts, the south coast would have very few people.

The south coast is too dry for most crops, but citrus fruits can **thrive** there. These fruits include lemons, oranges, and grapefruit. America's first navel oranges were grown along the coast in the early 1870s. Later, a California

Gravity pulls water through the aqueducts, over the hills of California, supplying water to the Los Angeles area.

grower developed the Valencia orange, which ripens in summer and fall. Since navel oranges ripen in winter, California could then produce citrus crops year-round. The area south of Los Angeles came to be called Orange County because it produced so many oranges.

Today, Orange County has only a few orange groves. Many farms did not survive because too many people wanted to live in the area.

As the value of land increased, many citrus growers decided to sell their farms. They moved north and east of Los Angeles, to Kern County and beyond. California still produces a great deal of citrus fruit. However, in Orange County, housing **developments** have replaced orange groves.

FISHING

California has rich **resources** in the sea, which borders the state's entire coast. The waters of the Pacific Ocean are full of fish and shellfish. Most of the catch is brought in by people who catch fish for money. Some of them work for big companies. Others are a part of family-owned businesses. The boats sail from ports in San Diego, Long Beach, Los Angeles, Santa Barbara, and San Luis Obispo. Fishers often use nets to capture fish by the ton. Some boats stay at sea for months, storing the fish on ice to keep them fresh.

A tugboat guides a container ship through the San Pedro Harbor.

California's biggest moneymaker now is **sea urchin.** Much of this catch is sold to Japan. There, people like the taste of it in sushi—a dish made of rice, seaweed, and raw fish.

Large numbers of anchovies are still harvested from the ocean. Anchovies measure only a few inches, but they run in **schools** of millions. Because of their strong flavor, anchovies are used more like a spice than a food. Tons of anchovies are also ground up and made into **fertilizer** or animal feed every year.

OCEAN RESOURCES

The ocean also supplies an important **mineral resource**—petroleum. Oil was first found in California on land that is now Los Angeles. When the oil wells ran dry, more oil was found offshore. Today, oil companies work from platforms out in the ocean. They pump oil from beneath the ocean floor. When they find oil or petroleum, they usually find a type of natural gas, too. This gas is the kind you might use as fuel for a camp stove.

Oil is found in sedimentary rock beneath the ocean floor.

The black goo that comes out of the ground is crude oil. It goes to nearby **refineries,** which separate the goo into useful products. Heating oil, petroleum jelly, plastic, and, above all, gasoline, are all made from crude oil.

California uses all the oil it produces and even buys more from other states and countries. California uses a great deal of energy because it is such a busy place. It produces more manufactured goods than any other state.

Rodeo Drive in Beverly Hills is a tourist attraction known for its designer clothing stores.

SOUTHERN CALIFORNIA INDUSTRIES

California factories make airplanes and airplane parts, spaceships, missiles, and weapons. They make medical equipment and scientific instruments. They make electronic goods such as video recorders and computers.

Los Angeles has a large clothing **industry.** Most of the actual sewing is done in Mexico and other countries. Southern California workers **design** the clothes, model them, advertise them, and handle the business details.

Surfing U.S.A.

Surfing is not just a sport but a lifestyle in southern California. It took off in the 1950s, when the modern lightweight surfboard was invented by a student at the California Institute of Technology. This billion-dollar industry is centered around San Diego and Orange Counties. Orange County now hosts many surfing competitions, including the "U.S. Open of Surfing."

The Myth of Hollywood

"Hollywood movies" are not really made in Hollywood anymore, but in other parts of Los Angeles. The real Hollywood was a small town where the movie **industry** was born. Now, it's a run-down neighborhood in Los Angeles that is slowly being **restored.**

Many of these jobs take years of technical training. The training is provided by private and public colleges and universities. The great private schools include the California Institute of Technology (Caltech), Stanford University, and the University of Southern California. The University of California is one of the public universities. It has **campuses** in Los Angeles, Davis, Santa Cruz, Berkeley, and eight other cities.

ENTERTAINMENT

One of the biggest industries in California is entertainment. Los Angeles is the **capital** of this industry in the United States. It is home to actors, directors, writers, performers, singers, and artists of every kind. It also has many workers with technical skills, such as camera operators and sound **engineers.** Most movies and many TV shows are made in southern California. From Los Angeles to San Francisco, there are many music recording studios, too.

Theme parks are another **profitable** entertainment business. Disney Studios started the trend with Disneyland **Resort.** Universal Studios followed with its movie park. Today, California has dozens of theme parks.

More than 14 million people visit Disneyland Resort in Anaheim every year.

LOS ANGELES

One third of all Californians live in the Los Angeles area. Los Angeles is the biggest city on the West Coast and the second biggest in the country. The city itself stretches 50 miles from north to south, and it has no clear boundaries. Los Angeles blends into Long Beach, which blends into the next city to the south, and so on. From any hilltop you can see sheets of one- or two-story buildings stretching over the horizon.

Most big cities have a crowded downtown area surrounded by more quiet neighborhoods. Los Angeles does not. Offices, factories, and businesses are found throughout the city. Los Angeles is really a collection of neighborhoods sewn together by freeways. Each neighborhood has its own busy sections. A few even have their own governments. Los Angeles has been called "a hundred

Los Angeles has sixteen major highways and about a dozen lesser ones that run throughout the city.

suburbs in search of a city," but that is not really correct. Los Angeles has world-class attractions similar to those of cities like New York, like big-league sports teams, important museums, and famous universities.

Los Angeles is a **diverse** city. People of many different **ethnic** groups live throughout the city. Some neighborhoods are especially known for an ethnic community. The *barrio* in east Los Angeles is largely **Latino.** Many African Americans live in Watts. The city also has large Filipino, Japanese, Chinese, and Korean neighborhoods.

Despite its wealth and importance, Los Angeles has serious problems. It has no subway system and the bus system is very limited. It is difficult to get around the city without cars. Freeways fill the landscape—and yet the freeways are often jammed. The many cars produce a lot of air pollution.

SAN DIEGO

The city of San Diego feels like a small town compared to Los Angeles. Actually, to the surprise of many, it ranks as the sixth largest city in the United States. Tourists flock to San Diego for the fine weather, clean air, warm ocean, and big surf.

On hot days, the mountains around Los Angeles trap the polluted air. It mixes with fog and becomes smog, a thick, yellow air that is hard to breathe.

Sunny days, warm water, and sandy beaches make surfing a popular sport.

Gigantic Balboa Park, in the middle of San Diego, contains a famous zoo with 800 **species** of animals on display. What makes this zoo special is the place itself. Animals do not live in cages, but in large areas built to look like their homes in nature. More than 3 million visitors to the zoo each year bring a lot of money into San Diego.

The military adds a great deal to the **economy** of this city as well. San Diego Bay is one of the world's great natural harbors. It is deep, and a long, skinny **peninsula** protects it from the ocean. That is why the country's largest naval base, San Diego Naval Base, is located here.

The Wild Animal Park

The San Diego Zoo operates the Wild Animal Park outside the city. Animals such as elephants and lions roam freely within these 2,200 fenced acres. To see the animals, people can ride through the park in a **monorail** that keeps them safe from the wild creatures. The zoo also offers tours.

California Transportation

Legend:
- ═══ Divided Highway
- ─── Other Highways
- ┼─┼ Railroad Lines
- ✈ Airports
- ⚓ Port cities

Highway 5 runs the length of the state, from Mexico to Oregon. Los Angeles has the busiest freeways, with more than six million cars on the road.

COMING AND GOING

Ships, trains, planes, and cars carry people and goods to and from California. San Pedro port in Los Angeles is the busiest port in the United States and the third busiest in the world. Oakland is a busy port as well. Through these and other California ports, goods flow to and from Asia. Cargo flows across the Mexican border, too, carried by trucks and trains. California leads the nation in the value of its trade.

The Central Valley

California's Central Valley is a great plain, 400 miles long and 50 miles wide. On a clear day, from the flat floor of the valley, you can see mountains on either side. The Sierra Nevada Mountains loom in the east like jagged teeth. In the west, you can see the gentle coastal hills. Within the valley, only a few peaks poke up here and there. They are the remains of ancient volcanoes.

Drive in any direction, however, and you come at last to hills. In the north, these hills mark the beginning of the Klamath range. In the south, the Tehachapi Mountains close the valley as they join with the curving tip of the Sierra Nevada. In short, mountains form a ring around the Central Valley.

In a **basin** like the Central Valley, water often forms salty lakes because it has nowhere to go. The Central Valley,

Modesto is in Stanislaus County, which brings in $1.3 billion for California in agricultural production each year.

29

California Central Valley Topography

14,495 ft
12,500 ft
10,000 ft
7,500 ft
5,000 ft
2,500 ft
Sea level

High Mountain

Goose Lake

Klamath Mts.

+ Mt. Shasta

Shasta Lake

+ Mt. Lassen

Arcata
Eureka

Redding

Sacramento River

Coastal

Sacramento

Lake Tahoe

San Francisco
Oakland
Stockton

Mono Lake

San Francisco Bay

San José

San Joaquin River

Sierra Nevada Mountains

Monterey

Fresno

Highest Elevation (14,495 ft.)
+

Central Valley

Lowest Elevation (-282 ft.)
+
Death Valley

Tulare Lake

Bakersfield

PACIFIC OCEAN

Santa Maria

Tehachapi Mountains

Desert

Colorado River Aqueduct

Santa Barbara

Los Angeles

Palm Springs

Long Beach

San Diego Aqueduct

Salton Sea

San Diego

N W E S

0   100 mi.
0   100 km

*The Central Valley is a level, broad, and **fertile** plain. It is home to the San Joaquin and Sacramento Rivers.*

however, has a drain. Its waters pour into the sea through one gap in the coast range—the San Francisco Bay.

RIVERS

Two great river systems drain this broad valley. The Sacramento River comes in from the north. It enters the valley near Mount Shasta and flows southwest to the San Francisco Bay. Along the way, smaller, swifter rivers feed into the Sacramento River. These rivers include the Yuba, the Feather, and the American.

Another set of roaring streams drains into the San Joaquin River system in the south. The San Joaquin River used to flow northwest and empty into the San Francisco Bay. Then, in the 1940s, too many **canals** began to draw water from it. Today, all of its water flows away into farms and fields. Not one drop of the San Joaquin River reaches the Pacific Ocean.

*Farmlands near the Sacramento River Valley benefit from nearby water and a good growing **climate**.*

CLIMATE

Summers in the Central Valley get extremely hot. Cool ocean breezes do not reach this area. Stockton can reach 100°F on a day when San Francisco, just 60 miles to the west, barely reaches 80°F. By July, only the **irrigated** lands in the valley look green. Everything else has turned golden brown.

Fall is short. Winter comes suddenly. A heavy ground mist called **tule fog** creeps over the Central Valley. Walking through tule fog is like flying through a cloud,

Irrigation machinery waters large fields by rolling across the land and spraying water.

California Water Plan

The California Water Plan is an **irrigation** system that carries water from man-made lakes north of the valley to farms at the southern end. Built in the 1960s, the **aqueducts, canals,** and dams move more water than any other system in the world.

because this fog may be 1,000 feet thick. Sometimes **tule fog** covers the entire Valley from Redding to Bakersfield. The Central Valley never gets snow, even though temperatures do sometimes drop below freezing.

FARMING

People are drawn to this area because of its rich soil. It is a mixture of sand, clay, and **silt.** Sand makes the soil airy. Clay helps it to hold water. Silt provides the food plants need to grow.

California's silt was built up over countless years by its two great river systems. Topsoil in the valley is 1,000 feet deep in places. The richness of the soil has led people to reshape the landscape. Lakes and **marshes** that once dotted the valley have been drained to create farms. The rivers in this region no longer follow the course set by nature. They have all been changed to meet the needs of farmers.

Farming is a big business in the Central Valley. Once owned by families, the **industry** has expanded to become **agribusiness,** run by large companies. Agribusiness companies use machines to plow, to plant, and to grow a wide variety of crops. They produce nuts such as almonds and walnuts. They grow apricots, avocados, grapes, olives, and other fruits. They grow vegetables such as Brussels sprouts, lettuce, artichokes, and herbs such as garlic.

When the crops ripen, machines are unable to pick them properly. **Migrant** workers do this job. Migrant

Central Valley California Resources

Natural Resources
- Oil
- Natural gas
- Borax
- Limestone
- Gold, silver
- Sand, gravel

Manufacturing
- Computers
- Clothing

Industry
- Forest products
- Fruit
- Grapes
- Rice
- Vegetables
- Olives
- Dairy products
- Cotton
- Sugar beets
- Cattle
- Walnuts
- Poultry
- Fish
- Skiing

0   100 mi.

workers move into an area when there is work and move on when the work is done. Many of California's migrants are people from Mexico.

California is the leading agricultural state in the United States. Many of the products are grown in the Central Valley.

Many cities in the Central Valley serve as farming **hubs.** Crops come into cities such as Fresno and Modesto from surrounding farms. Here, they are packaged for sale or made into products.

MINERAL RESOURCES

Petroleum and natural gas are important natural **resources** in the Central Valley. Both **minerals** are pumped out of the ground in the southern part of the Valley. Oil wells and **refineries** can be seen from Bakersfield to Stockton.

Natural gas in the Valley differs from that of southern California. In southern California, gas and oil are usually found together. This is called wet gas. In the Valley, however, natural gas is often found by itself. This so-called dry gas is the more useful type. It is used to fuel furnaces, water heaters, and stoves.

SACRAMENTO: THE STATE CAPITAL

The biggest city in the Valley revolves around quite a different business. Sacramento is the **capital** of California. It buzzes with the business of the state government. The state **capitol** and other government buildings form its center.

Sacramento was born around 1850, as a supply center for gold rush **miners.**

Old Sacramento State Historic Park is home to gold rush-era buildings that still look as they did back then.

The High Mountains

The Sierra Nevada Mountains are like a wall along 400 miles of the state's eastern border. The range has more than 500 peaks taller than 12,000 feet. The highest one, Mt. Whitney, touches the clouds at 14,495 feet above sea level. The only higher mountain in the United States is Alaska's Mt. McKinley.

The mountains continue north of the Sierra Nevada, but they belong to a different range called the Cascades. The Cascades were formed by hot liquid rock bursting out of the earth and piling up. The Cascades are actually a string of volcanoes from northern California to Canada. The biggest ones in California are Mount Shasta and Mount Lassen.

Mt. Whitney is located in Sequoia National Park, east of Fresno.

California High Mountain Topography

14,495 ft ►
12,500 ft ►
10,000 ft ►
7,500 ft ►
5,000 ft ►
2,500 ft ►
Sea level ►

High Mountain

Klamath Mts.
Goose Lake
+ Mt. Shasta
Arcata
Eureka
Shasta Lake
+ Mt. Lassen
Trinity Mts.
• Redding
Sacramento River
Lake Tahoe
Sacramento ★
Mono Lake
San Francisco •
• Oakland
San Joaquin River
Coastal
• San Jose
Sierra Nevada Mountains
Monterey •
Fresno •
Highest Elevation (14,495 ft.) +
Central Valley
Lowest Elevation (-282 ft.) +
Death Valley
Tulare Lake
PACIFIC OCEAN
Bakersfield •
Santa Maria •
Desert
Colorado River Aqueduct
Santa Barbara •
Los Angeles •
Palm Springs •
Long Beach •
San Diego Aqueduct
Salton Sea
San Diego •

N
W E
S

0   100 mi.

*California's mountain region offers visitors spectacular views, natural wonders, and **cultural** landmarks.*

Plate movements also created tall mountains in the north. The Klamath Range and Trinity Alps stretch from the Cascades to the coast.

SNOW IN CALIFORNIA?

Moist air from the ocean cools suddenly when it meets the high mountains and slides upward. The moisture then drops as rain or snow. On the western slopes of the Sierra, the snow can pile up to 50 feet deep in winter. The eastern slopes hardly get any rain or snow, because the air is dry by the time it gets there.

Winters are cold in the mountains. Rain in the valley usually means snow in the mountains. On the other hand, in the summer, when the **foothills** and valley are very hot, the mountains remain pleasantly cool. Not too many people live in the mountains, but thousands go there for **recreation.** Downhill skiing, snowboarding, snowmobiling, hiking, backpacking, hunting, and camping are all popular outdoor activities.

DESPERATE FOR WATER

The mountains provide more than fun in California. They provide life itself in the form of water. California usually gets no rain in the summer. Most of what falls in the winter runs off into the sea. The state depends on the snowpack in the mountains. The melting of this snow year-round creates rushing streams and rivers.

The rivers in the high mountains have all been **dammed** to create **reservoirs.** Cities all over the state get their drinking water from these reservoirs. Hetch Hetchy, for example, supplies San Francisco. Lake Berryessa supplies cities in the Valley. Los Angeles gets water from Mono Lake and from other lakes.

Shasta Dam, shown here, has enough concrete to build a three-foot-wide sidewalk around the world at the **equator.**

California High Mountain Resources

Natural Resources
- Oil
- Natural gas
- Borax
- Limestone
- Gold, silver
- Sand, gravel

Manufacturing
- Computers
- Clothing

Industry
- Forest products
- Fruit
- Grapes
- Rice
- Vegetables
- Olives
- Dairy products
- Cotton
- Sugar beets
- Cattle
- Walnuts
- Poultry
- Fish
- Skiing

The high mountain region provides many resources important for building.

Farmers also need the water for their fields. The cities want more for their ever-growing **suburbs.** Scientists, however, worry about life forms that die when dams are built and lands are flooded.

TREES

Trees are a major natural **resource** of the mountains. Timber brings in a lot of money. Giant redwood trees and Douglas firs cover the northern mountains and the western Sierra. Builders frame most wooden houses out of fir, so this wood is sold for a good price. Redwood has great value, too, because it does not easily rot when it gets wet. Decks, porches, and outdoor furniture are often made of redwood.

More than 90% of the original redwoods in California have been cut down by loggers.

VACATION PLACES

In the Gold Country of the Sierra **foothills,** gold mining towns like Sonora have been **restored.** Staying in these places is like living during the gold rush days.

Lake Tahoe calls itself the "jewel of the Sierra." It is a popular vacation place. Towns surrounding the lake are filled with shops and restaurants. Attractions include the lake itself, ski areas, and **gambling** in Nevada.

Lake Tahoe straddles the border of Nevada and California. It measures 21 miles from tip to tip and 12 miles across.

Desert and Basin

In one way, the landscape south of the Sierra is all the same: very dry and hot. Yet it offers great variety, too, with rocky ridges, sudden canyons, dry lake beds, and sandy **basins.**

DEATH VALLEY

The California desert may be divided into three areas: Death Valley, the Mojave Desert, and the Colorado Desert. Death Valley occupies the northeastern corner of this region. It is a deep canyon 140 miles long and up to 16 miles wide. It formed when a chunk of the earth's crust broke and sank.

During the gold rush, some travelers tried to enter California through Death Valley. Many died of thirst while crossing this blazing hot valley. The survivors named it Death Valley.

MOJAVE AND COLORADO DESERTS

South of Death Valley lies the Mojave Desert. Small

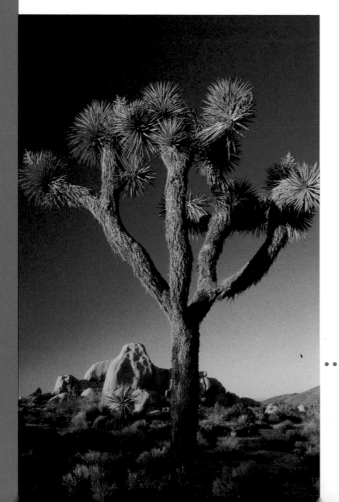

The Joshua tree has become a symbol of the Mojave Desert. It is able to survive in an area where most types of plant life cannot.

California Desert Topography

High Mountain
Goose Lake
Arcata
Eureka
Shasta Lake
Redding
Sacramento River
Lake Tahoe
Sacramento
San Francisco
Oakland
Mono Lake
Coastal
San Jose
San Joaquin River
Monterey
Fresno
Highest Elevation (14,495 ft.)
Death Valley
Lowest Elevation (-282 ft.)
Central Valley
Tulare Lake
Bakersfield
Santa Maria
Desert
Mojave Desert
Colorado River Aqueduct
PACIFIC OCEAN
Santa Barbara
Los Angeles
Palm Springs
Long Beach
San Diego Aqueduct
Salton Sea
Colorado Desert
San Diego

N W E S

0   100 mi.

Elevation scale
14,495 ft ▸
12,500 ft ▸
10,000 ft ▸
7,500 ft ▸
5,000 ft ▸
2,500 ft ▸
Sea level ▸

mountains break up the flat, sandy landscape. Long ago, the Mojave was part of the Pacific Ocean, but the rising coast range cut it off and turned it into a huge lake. Over time, the water **evaporated,** leaving dry lake beds and salty soil.

Several small mountain ranges block off the Colorado Desert from the Mojave Desert. The Colorado River runs through the eastern part of the Colorado Desert. The Salton Sea fills its southwestern corner. An **engineer** named

*25 million acres of California's deserts are publicly owned and include two national parks, one national **preserve,** six military bases, 72 wilderness areas, and 14 state parks.*

Smelly Water

The only water in Death Valley is found at Badwater. Here, a smelly liquid full of **minerals** bubbles out of a tiny spring. Badwater is 282 feet below sea level—the lowest point in North America.

Charles Rockwood created this **inland** sea by accident. In 1905, he was building some **irrigation canals** from the Colorado River. A flood broke the banks of one canal. The Colorado River poured into an ancient lake bed for two years, filling it with 83 feet of water. The water cannot drain out, so it keeps getting saltier.

RESOURCES

One might easily think of California's deserts as wastelands. In truth, they are full of valuable **resources.** For example, they have borax, a white salt-like **mineral.** Borax is an **additive** used to make detergents, gasoline, weed killers, insect killers, glass, and fire extinguishers. California mines over one million tons of borax every year—almost all of the world's supply.

Limestone is also found in the Mojave Desert. This white stone formed out of seashells millions of years ago. It is the key ingredient in Portland cement, made of sand, stone,

California Desert Resources

Natural Resources

- Oil
- Natural gas
- Borax
- Limestone
- Gold, silver
- Sand, gravel

Manufacturing

- Computers
- Clothing

Industry

- Forest products
- Fruit
- Grapes
- Rice
- Vegetables
- Olives
- Dairy products
- Cotton
- Sugar beets
- Cattle
- Walnuts
- Poultry
- Fish
- Skiing

Map labels: High Mountain, Arcata, Eureka, Redding, Sacramento, San Francisco, Oakland, Coastal, San Jose, Monterey, Fresno, Central Valley, Bakersfield, Santa Maria, Santa Barbara, Los Angeles, Long Beach, San Diego, Death Valley, Desert, Mojave Desert, Palm Springs, Colorado Desert, PACIFIC OCEAN

Scale: 0 ___ 100 mi.

Compass: N, W, E, S

and water. Portland cement in turn is the key ingredient in concrete. Other ingredients in concrete include sand and gravel. These are also mined by the trainload in the California deserts. By supplying the ingredients for concrete, the deserts have made a big difference to California. Concrete is necessary in almost every structure that is built, from skyscrapers to swimming pools.

Unlike other California deserts, the soil of the Colorado Desert is rich. The Colorado River, one of the biggest

*The desert and **basin** areas provide resources, like borax and limestone, which help create other products.*

43

rivers in the United States, runs through it. **Irrigation canals** tap its water to serve farms between the Salton Sea and the Mexican border. This area is called the Imperial Valley, and irrigation has made it bloom. Here, Californians grow alfalfa, cotton, fruit, sugar beets, lettuce, and many other crops.

A DESERT PARADISE

Palm Springs is the largest city in the California desert. It has about 45,000 people, but the population doubles in winter because of visitors. The main **industry** of this **resort** town is **recreation.** Golf courses, off-road driving tours, tennis, rock climbing, and hiking are all available year-round because of the favorable **climate.**

California is a state of great contrasts. Its four geographic regions offer different climates, landscapes, industries, and **resources.** Each region has met the challenges of its climate and **landforms,** and uses its resources to benefit all regions of California, as well as the rest of the world.

The Givenchy Hotel and Spa in Palm Springs has 2 indoor swimming pools, 22 treatment rooms, a hair salon, a gift shop, and a café.

Map of California

⊗	capital
•	cities
~	river
—	state line

High Mountain

Goose Lake

Arcata
Eureka

Shasta Lake

Redding

Sacramento River

Lake Tahoe

Sacramento ⊗

Mono Lake

San Francisco • Oakland

San Jose •

Coastal

San Joaquin River

Monterey •

Fresno •

Central Valley

Tulare Lake

Bakersfield •

Santa Maria •

Desert

Colorado River Aqueduct

Santa Barbara •

PACIFIC OCEAN

Los Angeles •

Long Beach •

Palm Springs •

San Diego Aqueduct

Salton Sea

San Diego •

N
W E
S

0   100 mi.

Washington

Oregon   Idaho

Nevada

Utah

Pacific Ocean

Arizona

MEXICO

Glossary

additive substance added to another in small amounts

agribusiness industry related to farming

aqueduct structure that carries water a long distance

basin area of land drained by a river and its branches

bay window window or set of windows that sticks out from the wall of a building

bioscience study of plants, animals, and other living things

campus grounds of a university or other school

canal artificial waterway

capital center of an industry; location of a government

capitol building in which the legislature meets

climate weather conditions that are usual for a certain area

cultural relating to the ideas, skills, arts, and a way of life of a certain people at a certain time

dammed having a barrier to hold back the flow of water

design to plan a thing to be made or built

development (housing) area of land with houses on it

diverse having variety

economy/economic means of bringing money to a region

engineer person who has charge of an engine or of machinery or technical equipment

equator imaginary circle around the Earth everywhere equally distant from the North and South Poles

ethnic belonging to a group with a particular culture

evaporate to change into a vapor

fertile bearing crops or vegetation in abundance

fertilizer material added to soil to make it more fertile

foothill low hills at the base of a mountain or mountain range

gable triangular part of an outside wall of a building formed by the sides of the roof sloping down

gambling playing a game in which something is risked

hub center of activity

industry group of businesses that offer a similar product or service

inland not near the sea coast

irrigate/irrigation supply water to land

landform natural feature of a land surface

Latino person from a Latin American country or who speaks Spanish; the term Hispanic is also sometimes used to describe such a person

marsh area of soft wet land usually overgrown with grasses and related plants

migrant farm laborer from another country who comes to work in the United States during a growing season

miner person who works in a mine

mineral solid substance formed in the earth by nature and obtained by mining

monorail single rail serving as a track for a wheeled vehicle

peninsula piece of land extending into a body of water

preserve keep or save from injury or ruin

profitable making money

recreation means of refreshing the mind and body

refinery place with machinery used to bring metals, oil, or sugar to a pure state

reservoir place where water is kept for future use

resort place where people go for pleasure

resource something that is available to take care of a need; there are natural and human-made resources

restore bring back to an original state

school large number of one kind of fish swimming together

sea urchin rounded shellfish related to starfish that lives on or burrows in the sea bottom and is covered in spines

silt particles left in water

souvenir something that serves as a reminder

species group of organisms that share the same physical characteristics

suburb city or town just outside a larger city; suburban means having to do with a suburb

symphony large orchestra of wind, string, and percussion instruments

thrive do very well

tourism industry built around people who travel for pleasure

tule fog heavy, dense fog found in marshy areas where tule reed and cat tails grow

turret little tower often at the corner of a building

urban relating to the city

vineyard place where grapevines are grown

More Books to Read

Harder, Dan. *A Child's California.* Portland, Oreg.: WestWinds Press, 2000.

Jaskol, Julie and Brian Lewis. *City of Angels: In and Around Los Angeles.* New York: Dutton Books, 1999.

Kennedy, Teresa. *California.* Danbury, Conn.: Children's Press, 2001.

Pelta, Kathy. *California.* Minneapolis, Minn.: Lerner Publications Company, 2001.

Index

agribusiness   32–33
airports   18
animal life   27
aqueducts   20, 34

Badwater   42
Balboa Park   27
Bay Area Rapid Transit
    (BART)   18
beaches   9, 14, 19, 21, 25,
    27
Berkeley   12, 15, 24
Big Sur   9, 19
borax   42, 43

California Water Plan   32
Caltrans system   18
Cascade Mountains   35–36
Catalina Island   19
Chinatown   14
climate   9–10, 19–20, 31–32,
    44
clothing industry   23
Colorado Desert   8, 40–41,
    43
Colorado River   20, 41, 42,
    43

Death Valley   8, 40, 42
deserts 8, 40–44
Disneyland Resort   24

earthquakes   6, 10
economy   8
entertainment industry   18,
    24

farming   10–11, 32–33
fishing industry   21–22

gold rush   13, 34, 39, 40
Golden Gate   12, 15, 18

Haight Ashbury   15
Hetch Hetchy reservoir   37
Highway 5   28
Hollywood   24
housing developments   21

Imperial Valley   44
Industrial Light and Magic
    18
irrigation   30, 31, 42, 44

Klamath mountain range   29,
    36

Lake Berryessa   37
Lake Tahoe   39
limestone   42
Los Angeles   5, 21, 22, 23,
    24, 25–26, 28, 37

manufacturing   22
Marin County   18
migrant workers   32–33
mining   39
Mojave Desert   8, 40–41, 42
Mono Lake   37
Monterey Bay   9, 19
Mount Lassen   35
Mount Shasta   30, 35
mountains   5, 7, 9–10, 19,
    26, 29, 35–39, 41
Mt. Whitney   35

Napa Valley   11
natural resources   10–11, 34,
    38

Oakland   12, 16, 18, 28
Orange County   21, 23

Palm Springs   44
Petaluma   11
petroleum industry   22, 34
population   4
ports   21, 28

reservoirs   37
rivers   13, 20, 30–31, 32, 37,
    41, 42, 43, 44
Rockwood, Charles   42

Sacramento   34
Sacramento River   13, 30, 31
Salton Sea   41–42
San Diego   5, 20, 21, 26–27
San Francisco   10, 11, 12–15,
    18, 24
San Francisco Bay   13, 30, 31
San Joaquin River   30, 31
San Jose   5, 12, 16, 17
San Pablo Bay   13
San Pedro port   28
Santa Barbara Islands   19
Sierra Nevada   8, 20, 29, 35
Silicon Valley   17
Sonoma Valley   11
Sonora   39
Stanford University,   24
state capital   34
surfing   23

Tehachapi Mountains   29
theme parks   24
tourism   5, 6
transportation   18, 28
Trinity Alps   36
tule fog   31–32

Universal Studios   24
University of California   15,
    24

Victorian houses   13–14
vineyards   11
volcanoes   10, 29, 35

Watts   26
Wild Animal Park   27

About the Author

Tamim Ansary lives in San Francisco, California. He has worked for twenty years as a textbook editor and writer. His nonfiction series for children include *Holiday Histories* and *Native Americans.* Currently, he writes a learning column for Encarta Online.